Within: Life, Love, And Liberty

James Alden

BookLeaf
Publishing

India | USA | UK

Made with ❤ on the BookLeaf Publishing Platform

www.bookleafpub.in

www.bookleafpub.com

Dedication

For my wife, my daughters, and my son—
whose love, strength, and memory inspire every page.

Preface

In the quiet moments between the rush of life, there are the questions that linger, the truths we confront, and the emotions that define us. In *Within: Life, Love, and Liberty*, I invite you into a journey—a journey that touches upon the ebb and flow of existence, the complexity of love in all its forms, and the sacrifice and pride of standing for liberty. These poems are not just words on a page; they are reflections of what it means to be human, to feel deeply, and to strive for something greater than oneself.

Life—a force that cannot be contained, only lived, with all its seasons, joys, struggles, and fleeting moments. Life is in the turning of a page, the quiet of the morning, the fire in our bones that drives us forward. It is growth and loss, birth and death, a continuous loop that shapes who we are, what we become, and what we leave behind.

Love—the most powerful force we'll ever know, yet the most fragile. It transcends boundaries, from the unbreakable bond of family to the quiet depth of friendship. It is in the first glance, the last goodbye, and the quiet spaces in between. Love is where we find meaning, comfort, pain, and healing—often all at once. And it is within love that we find our truest selves, if we allow it.

Liberty—the breath of freedom, the weight of sacrifice. It is the foundation of this nation, the fire that lit the path for generations before us, and the guiding light for those who fight to preserve it. For some, liberty comes with the price of war, the toll of loss, and the ongoing battle to protect what is ours. For others, it's a gift handed down through time, something we must honor and uphold with every step. It is the unshakable belief in a cause greater than ourselves.

In these pages, you will find pieces of who I am and who I was—capturing the beauty and pain of these themes, exploring them through the lens of my experiences, my joys, my sorrows, and my battles. Some poems are quiet, some are loud, some are filled with hope, while others are drenched in grief. But each word holds a part of my story, a part of what it means to be *within* the human experience.

As you read, I hope you will find echoes of your own life, your own loves, and the liberties you hold dear. These poems are for those who have lived, loved, and fought—whether on a battlefield, in the heart, or in the quiet spaces of life. They are for those who know the struggle, the triumph, and the meaning that comes from truly being alive.

This is my story. These are my words. And now, they are yours.

Acknowledgements

To my wife, Cassidy, whose patience, insight, and unwavering support have been my anchor throughout this entire process. Your belief in me—especially when I doubted myself—has made this work possible.

To my family, whose love and encouragement have been the foundation of this journey. You never stopped believing in me, and for that, I am endlessly grateful. Your strength and inspiration are woven into every word of this book.

A special thank you to BookLeaf Publishing, whose creativity and dedication transformed my vision into something tangible. Your team's professionalism and attention to detail have made this book something I am proud to share with the world.

This book is dedicated to the brave men and women I had the honor to serve alongside. Their sacrifices, courage, and camaraderie have inspired the poems within these pages. You are forever in my heart.

Finally, to everyone who has supported, read, and shared their thoughts on this collection—thank you for being part of this journey. This book is as much yours as it is mine.

1.

Saffron paints the parchment of the sky,
As the sun lessens its fiery gaze.
Youthful green surrenders itself
To the golden wisdom of age.
The rustle of drying leaves,
Every bough an artist,
Dressing the forest in a tapestry
Of crimson, amber, scarlet, and bronze.
An orchestral symphony
Meant to warm our souls,
Playing not to the ears
But to the eyes, the heart, the spirit.
A prelude to slumber,
To winter's serene silence,
The beckoning of its icy embrace.
Morning mists hang low,
Preparing the world for a spectacle
A curtain to rise and unveil
That even in decay
Resides beauty.

2.

Under the weight of time, a struggle unfolds,
a tapestry of joy and sorrow,
threads woven tight, frayed at the edges.

Mountains of ambition loom,
valleys of defeat stretch wide.
Faith and doubt entwine.
A candle flickers,
its fragile light a testament to the fight within.

The heart pounds with echoes of triumph,
echoes of wounds.
Each step forward, a silent scream of will.

Standing tall,
through storms and trials,
man rises or he falls.
Every broken piece,
every shattered dream,
a chance to choose his path.

To forfeit grit, a shattered mast
or press on and fortify.

Though the journey is hard,
the nights long,
the heart weary,
a steadfast song beats on.
In the ebb and flow of life's relentless tide,
the spirit endures,
unbroken.

3.

Hidden behind a bare reflection.

I've been molded, carved, and turned,
by forces I could not resist.
I am shaped each day like clay,
but mine are not the potter's hands.

I am the vessel left to crack.

The hollow space I never chose,
now holds what others have thrown.
Washing away all that I was,
and all I longed to be.

A final plea to all that's lost.

I speak in borrowed voices,
in tongues I've never learned.
I feel the whispers scrape my throat,
their scars echoed in my choice.

I stumble ahead with barren hands.

I tread a path I never set,
on feet too unfamiliar.
Each and every wavering step,
muffled deeper by the question.

Who am I, when I was never me?

4.

The forest holds me still,
like the breath before a storm.
Soft branches envelop me,
muting the world around.

But beneath the leaves, the darkness calls,
the echoes of all that was hidden,
and I am forced to listen,
for I cannot move.

The quiet grows too loud,
boughs begin to squeeze,
a tightening in my chest,
the weight of truth untold.

The cavern within is echoing,
filling the air with unsaid words,
every whisper now a shout,
a storm in my mind that cannot be quelled.

Here, in this place of stillness,
as bound by the silence, I am,
the very thing I sought to escape.
The forest no longer shelters me,
but what will not bend, shall break.

Swiftly now, I turn away,
snapping the ties that bind.
Silently, they fall behind,
to be faced another day.

I collect my shattered pieces,
and shove them deeper still,
far deeper than before,
fragments of thought once held.

With bated breath, I lock them away,
buried under plaster smiles.
Tighter and tighter, I tie them,
until I believe I've won.

On I walk, as if at peace,
the calm only surface deep,
while pressure scratches beneath my skin,
begging to be unleashed.

It rattles in its cage I've built,

but these chains I wear, I chose,
pretending the storm has passed again,
until the forest calls me home.

5.

Venomous words fill the air,
You are nothing but the sum of your mistakes.
Another lie to feed the flames,
You'll never be enough.
Burning the walls within to ash,
Failures stack like bricks.
A drum beating against my ribs,
You'll crush the ones you love.
A storm churning in my chest,
You're defined by what you've broken.
The weight of secrets buried deep,
Some things can't be forgiven.
Each mistake echoes louder than the last,
Your shame will follow you forever.
Shadows twist in every thought,
You can never escape who you were.
A cold grip tightens around my heart,
Who could love what you've become?
But beneath the pain, something stirs,
What if there's room to heal?

The voice of doubt starts to fray,
You are more than the lies revealed.
A crack in the armor, soft but real,
You are worthy of new beginnings.
Through the darkness, a flicker grows,
Even broken things can be made whole.
The past may never fade...
Then piece by piece, I'll rise again.

6.

A wave replaced a wave.
The sand beneath laid in a new pattern,
softer, sharper, unfamiliar.
Will this, too, pass?
Or is this now my shape?

I looked for it, the part of me I knew,
That small fragment I thought was mine.
My hand laid bare, I grasped at nothing,
The pieces shifting like water.

Footprints fade as quickly as they form,
The tide rolls in, erasing all behind me.
Smoothed and shifted by wind and wave,
Each step a whisper of change.

Salt spray lands on skin anew,
Redefined by the ocean's breeze.
With the shifting of the sands I'm altered,
A wave replaced a wave.

7.

For a moment, everything stops.

The chatter,
The rush,
The endless cycle of noise.

I breathe.
The breath I forgot I was holding.
My heart begins to settle.

For that one suspended moment,
I am still.
Caught in the space between worlds.

I feel the ground beneath my feet,
The hum of life, distant.
But not mine,
Not for now.

Not in this moment,

This brief respite.
My time belongs to me,
Once more.

8.

Without Knowing
You have possessed me.
Your soul has entered mine,
And touched its darkest places.

Without Seeing
You have engulfed my heart,
You have ignited a passion within.

Without Hearing
You have enchanted me,
Your siren song has lured me in.

Without Feeling
You have led me,
Your guidance has been my blinding beacon.

Without Speaking
You have whispered wisdom,
Your actions have inspired me to dream.

Without Trying
You have saved me,
Your love has been as Angel's wings.

A light that lifts me higher,
A force that brings me peace.

9.

Your love is the calm amidst the storm,
In a sea of endless motion.

Without you, I would be adrift,
My vessel would tilt unanchored.

Mine would be an aimless life,
Floating among the wreckage
Of fools like me.

You are my reason,
My home and port.

You are my hope,
My compass and map.

You are my strength,
My tide and sail.

You are my lighthouse,
Which guides me home.

10.

How fortunate are we
To carry the weight of loss.

To wrestle with grief,
To dwell in mourning,
To harbor sorrow,
To endure agony.

How fortunate are we
To have felt so deeply.

To have loved so fiercely,
To have treasured so dearly,
To have cherished so profoundly,
To have prized so wholly.

And yet,

How fortunate are we,
That the love that's gone can echo

Through the caverns of our hearts
Until its final beat.

Left not in emptiness,
But resonance of love,
A love that lives on,
Tender, fierce,
Ever lasting, ever brief.

How fortunate are we.

11.

He followed with childlike wonder,
So he could lead with wisdom.

His whimsy carries shadows,
Of the boy he used to be.
Now his words of reason,
Are reason enough for words.

There is peace in his presence,
His hand steadies storms within.
The scent of strength and sandalwood,
Stifles notes of sorrow.
His laughter quiets loneliness,
Giving promise of tomorrow.
His embrace evokes calm,
Evicting cruelty with ease.
His timber tempers troubles,
Pain forbade upon his tone.

All of this because he learned to lead with wisdom,
By following in childlike wonder.

12.

She walks softly,
Her fingers brushing the earth,
Awakening what was lost,
Stirring the stillness of a frigid embrace.

She whispers in the quiet dark,
Where the frozen seeds have slept,
And with the warmth of her breath,
She calls life back from the edges of silence.

From the soil, like a prayer,
A flower begins to bloom.
A tender bud unfurls its face,
To the sun's first kiss.

You, my love, are that delicate blossom,
A promise of light in shadow.

The gentle winds carry your name,
And in their sweet breeze, I hear the echo

Of love reawakened,
Of hearts reborn,
Of hope that rises like long night's dawn.

She gathers strength in your growth,
Her warmth in the curve of your tiny form,
Her song in the flutter of your heart,
And in this season she shows us
That love, once lost, can return.

For in your coming,
We are remade,
Hearts reunited,
With love eternal.

13.

In every tender gaze, a universe unfolds,
A mother's love, a story yet untold.
With hands that soothe and hearts that mend,
She guides with grace until the very end.

In whispered lullabies, dreams take flight,
Underneath her watchful, loving light.
Her embrace, a harbor in life's stormy sea,
A haven of warmth where little ones flee.

With laughter like sunlight, she fills each day,
Painting memories in hues of joyous play.
Her patience endless, her kindness pure,
In her arms, all fears find their cure.

In every sacrifice, her love is shown,
A quiet strength, a cornerstone.
For in her, the world finds its nurture,
A beacon of love, unwavering and sure.

So here's to the woman, both gentle and strong,
Whose love and care will forever belong.
A tribute to the mother, in every way,
Who makes our world brighter, day by day.

14.

We walk not side by side,
But as twin flames,
Pushing toward the same horizon.

You saw my limits,
Before I knew what they were,
And with quiet strength,
You urged me to break them.

You pull me toward rapids,
Where currents run deep,
Where rocks are sharp,
But the view from the other side,
Is a place I never thought to reach.

I, too, hold a mirror to you,
Reminding you of the strength you hide,
Of dreams long buried,
Beneath the weight of the world.

We speak not in promises,
But in challenges,
Knowing that to grow,
We must embrace risk.

For a love that stirs,
Does not shelter, but stirs,
In quiet and storm,
Is the threads woven tight.
The fabric of each other's becoming.

15.

Streaks of Crimson unfurl.
Bloodshed.
Each drop an offering to prosperity.

Eruptions of White hot flames erupt.
Purifying.
Cleansing the innocent of their chains.

A field of Sapphire overwhelms the skies above.
A promise.
The canopy of Truth that never wanes.

A symbol of courage,
Steadfast and vigilant.
A beacon of hope,
Rising with the dawn.
A silent song of glory,
Carried on eagle's wings.

16.

I stand in my place,
With my feet firm below,
My head held up high,
And the clock seems to slow.

I scribble my name,
To be all I can be,
No matter the cost,
For the Land of the Free.

My chest pounds with the weight,
Of an Oath to defend,
From within, or without,
To protect, till the end.

I raise my right hand,
And vow to uphold,
The flag of our fathers,
Red, white, blue, and bold.

Freedom is paid for,
With blood, sweat, and brass,
So, I'll rise up with pride,
And defend till my last.

17.

The sun rises over the mountains,
Painted in hues of fire and blood.
Dust lingers in the air,
Shadows of the men we once were,
But no longer are.

Gunfire splits the sky,
Ripping the morning apart,
Like paper in the hands of a child,
Loud. Sharp. Unforgiving.
The enemy falls,
But so do we.

I hear his breath,
A final shudder in the dust,
It's the man right beside me,
The one who had a laugh,
Like thunder in the barracks,
Now swallowed by this endless war.

The horizon doesn't blink.
It keeps burning,
Like the pain in my chest,
The hole in my soul,
The mission is clear:
Survive, kill, repeat.
No one tells you,
How to carry the dead,
When the battle is done.

18.

The night stretches longer
Than I ever thought it could.
The stars are silent,
With their cold, indifferent eyes,
Staring down into my soul,
Unmoved by the weight of the world.

I sit silently in the dark,
Finger stiff upon my arms.
I watch the moonlight shadows move,
Or, maybe, it's my mind.
It plays its cruel, sly tricks,
No shots,
No screams,
Only the faintest hum,
Of my heartbeat in the silence.

The watch feels endless,
The crisp wind brings nothing.
Nothing but a night,

That refuses to give.

The only sound I hear,
Is the pulsing in my ears,
Thumping louder than the thoughts,
I cannot seem to drown.

How did I get here?
Why do we fight?
What do we wait for?
The stillness of the world,
Stirs the questions in my head,
That I don't have the answers for.

19.

Sand.
Mud.
Rain.
Snow.

Brothers in arms,
We bled together.
Never asked why,
Just when, check Roger.

Fall into dirt,
Step in time.
No last words,
A silent goodbye.

Fight.
Kill.
Bleed.
Die.

Even warriors fall,
And the ones left behind,
Are the only ones there,
To bear the weight of it all.

I carry it anyway,
For you,
For me,
For us,
For them.
Because that's what we do.

At ease, carry on.

20.

The barracks are empty,
Only echoes remain.
In the hall,
In the stairs,
In my head,
In the wall.

But the silence is full,
So heavy, like dust.
From my boots,
From my clothes,
From my skin,
From my brain.

It's always in the quiet,
That the memories are loudest.
The stillness carries ghosts,
I no longer wish to hear.

21.

Now, I'm just a man.
Catching flashes of you,
In the quiet of the day,
Like a home that wasn't lost,
But now the world feels strange,
There are spaces in these boots,
That I just cannot fill.

Now, I'm just a man.
Who thought I left behind the fight,
But in the silence, you're still here,
Reminding me, it's not my life,
Pulling memories from my hair,
Casting shadows on the wall.

Now, I'm just a man.
In a world that doesn't know me,
Fighting a war no one can see,
Stuck between the man I was,
And who, again, I'll never be.

Peace is just a battle,
For just a man like me.